the house book

A comprehensive guide to
making a home

the

house

book

p

This is a Parragon Book
First published in 2002

Parragon
Queen Street House
4 Queen Street
Bath BA1 1HE
United Kingdom

Created and produced by The Bridgewater
Book Company Ltd, Lewes, East Sussex

Creative Art Director Stephen Knowlden
Art Directors Colin Fielder, Sarah Howerd,
Michael Whitehead, Johnny Pau
Editorial Director Fiona Biggs
Editorial Mark Truman, Sarah Yelling, Sarah Doughty
Photographers Steve Gorton, Alistair Hughes,
Steve Tanner

ISBN: 0-75259-053-7

Printed in China

Contents

COLOUR IN YOUR HOME

MAKING SOFT FURNISHINGS

The house book

The House Book has four sections. Beginning with Home Decorating, the first section will show you how to transform your home. Colour In Your Home then guides you through the world of colour schemes available for you and your home. Designing New Rooms gives you inspiration for transforming every room in your house. Finally, the section on Making Soft Furnishings will help you to add comfort and style to your home.

PART 1

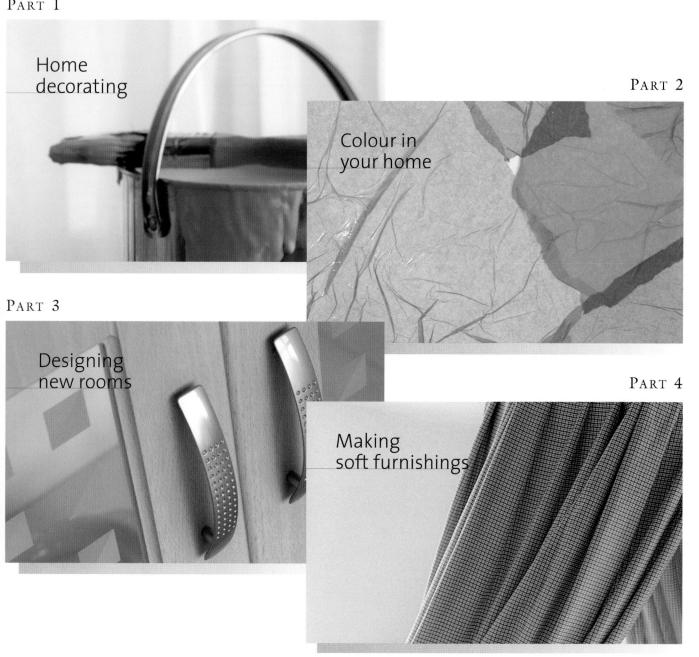

Home
decorating

PART 2

Colour in
your home

PART 3

Designing
new rooms

PART 4

Making
soft furnishings

The house book

Introduction

Whether you are an expert looking for bright ideas to give your home a fresh new look, or a complete beginner requiring basic information on decorating, The House Book is the book for you.

The walls in this sitting room have been painted porcelain blue with a white glaze swirled in.

Part 1: Home Decorating

This section will enable you to make a professional job of all your decorating tasks. There are tips to help you to plan the job properly and work out your budget. You'll need to decide on colour schemes and the kind of paint to use – guidance is given to help you choose from the countless varieties now available on the market.

Painting techniques are described in detail and you'll find suggestions for interesting effects to give your rooms a special look. These methods include sponging, colourwashing and textured paint. However, if you decide to hang wallpaper instead you'll find it's not as difficult as you might think, as long as you plan the work carefully and accurately.

Perhaps you hope to make a radical change to the look and feel of your home by removing plaster to reveal the original brickwork, laying handmade tiles or creating your own wood panelling. Everything you need to know is covered here, from the basics about wood and bricks to decorative effects using mosaics and mirrors.

Flooring is a vital part of your home makeover. Here you will find practical advice on choosing materials wisely, depending on your budget and the uses of each room. A section is dedicated to woodwork, which includes basic painting skills along with special effects such as crackleglazing, and instructions for french polishing.

Once the decorating is completed, look up the clever storage tips and ideas for livening up your accessories and making the best use of the space available.

Part 2: Colour In Your Home

This section is full of inspiring ideas to make your home more attractive. The information on colour theory explains why some colours blend comfortably together while other colours clash, creating visual friction. With this in mind, you'll be able to use your instinctive colour preferences in a sensible combination and have the satisfaction of creating a home using your preferred colour schemes.

The chapter on the influence of colour demonstrates how the colours you choose can have a significant effect on your state of mind. Aqua and turquoise can be calming, while pale pink has a soothing effect.

If you're brave you may go for a strong colour, such as orange, a great favourite with professional interior designers. Yellow is an inviting, sociable colour that suits a contemporary style of décor.

Paint effects are making a comeback, so let your imagination run wild. There are ideas on how to create simple, fun effects, such as stencilling, and produce clever 3-D effects with colour. Applied textures are also fashionable – why not consider lining your walls with a natural material such as cane or bamboo?

Perhaps you want to renew your home in a particular style. Think about which theme fits best with your lifestyle: a country feel, with soft, muted colours; or maybe the rich, earthy colours of a Tuscan farmhouse. Maybe you are a more of an urban minimalist, preferring a limited colour palette and a clutter-free environment. Or go further afield for inspiration, looking to Morocco or India for rich, intense colours to liven up your rooms.

Use of a bold colour on nearly every surface may not appeal to everyone as a decorating option. If the colour is applied with confidence, however, the results can be stunning, and certainly make a strong statement, often reflecting the personality of a room's occupant.

Part 3: Designing New Rooms

This section takes you through the process of revamping your home, room by room. Decide whether to go for the traditional or the contemporary look, and take it from there. Don't despair if you can't afford to rip out that old kitchen and start from scratch. There are many ways of ringing the changes in an economical way. Try fixing new doors on your kitchen units or even simply replacing the handles.

The sitting room is the public face of your home, so show off your personal style. You could go for a traditional look, with heavy bookshelves and comfortable sofas or an uncluttered minimalist look. If you have a sitting-dining room, try defining the dining area with low walls or screens to reinforce the fact that the room serves two different purposes. Or if you're lucky enough to have a separate dining room, look up the imaginative ideas for flooring, lighting and furniture that will make the most of it.

By simply removing cupboard doors from a plain base unit and using willow baskets on the shelves as pull-out drawers, you can give a room a completely new country look.

The bedroom, the least public room of the home, is the perfect place to express yourself but don't spoil the effect with clutter; keep it at bay with some sensible storage methods. When you decorate the kids' bedrooms, take into account their basic needs for study, play and relaxation in a safe, comfortable environment and make sure you involve them in your decision-making!

The chapter on bathrooms helps you to create a practical design in a traditional or contemporary style, with ideas for shower rooms and en suite showers. Then consideration is given to creating a perfect home-office environment, neatly designed to take up minimum space yet with comfort in mind.

Part 4: Making Soft Furnishings

This section is full of ideas for using fabric to enhance your living space. There are projects for both the novice and the experienced needleworker. Fabrics and trimmings are described, along with explanations of equipment and haberdashery.

Ready-made curtains are expensive, so why not make your own? Go for a modern style, such as tab-top curtains, or the traditional swag and tails. If you're a beginner, start with a simple unlined pair. Instructions for making all the accessories and for creating your own blinds are included too. Think twice before buying new furniture – it's easy to revitalise your chairs and sofas by changing the fabric. Ensure you have enough seating for all your visitors by making your own cushions or bean-bag chairs or give a deckchair a new lease of life for outdoors. At mealtimes, impress your guests with hand-made table linen and napkins, a simple but very effective soft-furnishing project that anyone with even the most basic needleworking skills can attempt with confidence.

A colourful border can make an ordinary sheet into a special item of bed linen.

Storage is always a problem especially in small flats or town houses. Consider making beautiful fabric bags, lined baskets and clothes covers to remove clutter from your bedroom. Improve your bedroom further by making your own bedding. It's not as hard you might think. Not only is it economical, you can use exactly the colour and fabric that you desire and personalise it by hand-embroidering your own decorative motifs. Go to town with piles of cushions in luxurious fabrics, bordered sheets or for a special change, make a dramatic bedspread that becomes a centrepiece of your bedroom.

Finally, there are ideas for decorative touches – the braid, trimmings, bows or rosettes that make your soft-furnishing project really special.

Home decorating

Introduction

As the world enters a new millennium, people's lives have never been more stressful, their workstyles more fractious and time specific, or their complex lifestyles more fragmented.

Carefully chosen calm and soothing colours will ensure that your bedroom is a relaxing place in which to spend your time.

Consequently, relaxation at the end of a difficult day has become more of a basic requirement than ever before, and to be able to wind down in comfort and style in aesthetically pleasing decorative surroundings is not so much a bonus as a necessity.

Relaxing in familiar surroundings usually involves personal input to the area in question; favourite colours and textures, controllable lighting systems, displays and pictures and mementoes all act as a 'welcome home'. Whether the 'home' is owned, mortgaged or rented or whether it is a house, cottage or flat, the decorative personal touch is essential if home is to be where the heart is.

Employing third parties to do decorating work is expensive, and it is indeed time-consuming finding the right people for the job. The work that is done for you still requires a lot of personal input and it carries no real guarantees of workmanship. So instead, why not channel the energies of personal attention into the task itself?

There are important points to bear in mind, however. You will always need to be aware of the possible complexity of the task, whether it is merely deciding on colour schemes for walls or whether it involves a complete makeover, in line with those shown so regularly on television.

In order to retain viewer interest, DIY programmes edit down technical job sequences from hours to seconds. This could lead the unwary or naive into the erroneous belief that a decorating job can be done in the time it takes on television.

The most important function of this book is to bring a sense of reality to the initial discussions and scheduling, allowing decorating decisions to reflect a proper timescale, and to take into account the available skill levels and budget for the project.

Throughout these pages a proper professional approach is encouraged, from the drawing up of a detailed plan to the application of top quality materials and power tools in a safe and

responsible manner. The tools required are discussed at the start of each chapter, and step-by-step sequences show each job in progression, and can be easily followed and understood.

Whether these pages help with a simple painted frame or a complex zonal plan, hopefully, after it is completed, you will experience much greater satisfaction in having done a quality job in the home, rather than paying to have one done.

Choosing and fitting your own wallpaper is not a complicated job, as long as you follow some simple guidelines and do the preparation work correctly.

Planning

In today's highly competitive consumer-orientated marketplace, modern businesses must have carefully considered strategies and working schedules to ensure their survival and growth. You are probably aware of this requirement in your own daily working life and the same is no less true of planning home improvements. Most households already have some kind of general strategy for running the home smoothly, varying from a basic task 'duty roster' on a kitchen notice board to a complex time-specific system that includes family members and budgets, all logged onto a home computer. Forward planning is an essential part of running a home and is equally vital when it comes to making improvements, whether major or minor.

Practical considerations

No matter how small the job appears to be, forward planning is needed when you are considering refurbishing or decorating your home. Inspiration gained from a magazine or television 'makeover' needs to be turned into a plan of action if home improvement is to be successful. Here are some tips on what to think about before you start.

Clear brief

Imagine you have an independent builder taking on the job. What he would expect from his client is a clear brief, detailing all that is required from the finished work, which materials are going to be used and which colour scheme is required. Just because you intend to tackle the project yourself, don't skimp on the details when devising the plan of action. And beware: 'making it up as you go along' is liable to end in unsatisfactory results.

Questions to consider

Whether you live alone or with others, it is worth considering the following questions:

- Is the planned change suitable for the particular room that you have in mind?

- Is it practical?
- Will everyone in the house benefit?
- How long will it take?
- How much upheaval will there be?
- Can you live with it in the long term?

Budget

If the household members like the ideas and are happy to live with the works in progress, then you need to consider:

- How much will it cost?
- Is it affordable?

The job budget involves the adding of prices from builders' and decorators' lists, the cost of any new tools required and delivery charges for materials and/or rubbish clearance.

When planning a refurbishment, seek inspiration from a variety of sources, including magazines. Measure the room, draw a plan, and collect colour cards, paint testers and material swatches.

Skills and time

Presuming a reasonable skill level with a basic tool kit (the skills and tools required for each job are discussed throughout this book), try to devise a logical order of work, bearing in mind the following factors:

- The amount of work needed each day will depend on the size of the project, but don't take on too much in one go. Popular decorating programmes on television may give the impression that a room can be completely transformed in a mere 25 minutes, including a commercial break, but this is far from being the truth.
- Be realistic in assessing how long you think each part of the project will take.
- Cutting corners on any part of a job may lead to difficulties later on and may ultimately add to the time the job takes.

Implications of refurbishment

The eventual resale value of your property is not the only thing to bear in mind when assessing standards of workmanship. Removing period features from a room for 'modernisation' generally does not meet with approval today, so consider all the implications before you start. Sympathetic decorating and subtle changes can sometimes be more beneficial than wholesale refurbishment.

In years to come, you may tire of the changes you have made and seek to reinstate an earlier look, but if you have disposed of vital features, you may encounter considerable difficulty in replacing them. Give yourself time to come to terms with your plans; put them away for a while, then come back to them and reconsider what you have thought about. Don't be afraid to change your mind or tone down some of the more ambitious aspects of the project.

BEFORE

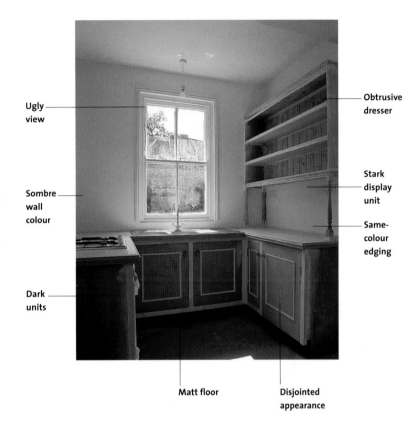

Ugly view

Sombre wall colour

Dark units

Obtrusive dresser

Stark display unit

Same-colour edging

Matt floor

Disjointed appearance

AFTER

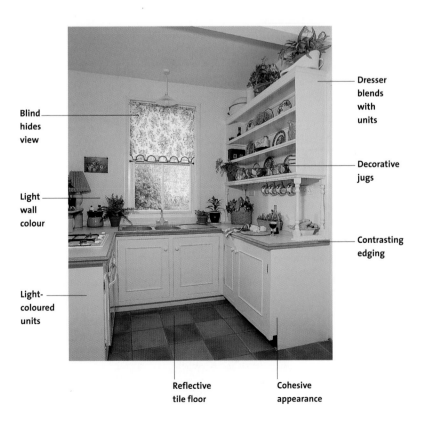

Blind hides view

Light wall colour

Light-coloured units

Dresser blends with units

Decorative jugs

Contrasting edging

Reflective tile floor

Cohesive appearance

Assessing room functions

If your work is not confined to one room and a complete makeover of the house is needed, then your plans must be more elaborate. Maybe you've just moved in or your family circumstances have changed dramatically. Whatever the reason, the first step is to assess the basic areas – living, working and sleeping – plus the role of the kitchen and bathroom.

Living areas

The living room must cater for all members of the household, who will use it for different reasons. Its main function is to provide a seating arrangement for family and friends where privacy is not possible. Several activities may take place in this room simultaneously, for example, reading, listening to music or watching television, family discussions and hobby pursuits, such as playing computer games. Decide whether an open-plan style is in keeping with this lack of privacy, or whether a breakdown of the living room into two separate functional areas is possible. In a period house, the downstairs living areas would usually have been arranged as a day room, near the cooking area for convenience, with easily cleaned flooring, and a separate evening area, with more luxurious fixtures and fittings, suitable for entertaining.

Working areas

What constitutes work, and what doesn't, may present an ever-changing issue in the contemporary household. Computers are used for schoolwork, business and family leisure activities. Digital interactive cables have transformed the television into a potential shopping mall and banking service. As certain areas become multi-functional, a study or home office may be a welcome retreat. This is a real necessity if you work from home full time; otherwise, professional commitments can easily spill over into everyday family life.

Sleeping areas

The younger members of a household often consider their bedroom space to be out of bounds to anyone not specifically invited. These areas are already catering for several activities, and must be furnished accordingly. The bedroom

Living areas often benefit from being divided into separate areas for different functions.

used solely for its intended purpose is usually the parents' room, traditionally the largest. Consider the benefits of young children sharing this room instead. It will double as a nursery or play area, possibly freeing up a room elsewhere in the house. A good night's rest, however, relies on peace and quiet, so the location of bedrooms away from sources of noise is very important.

The kitchen

Generally the working hub of the home, the kitchen is frequently in use for food preparation, cooking, washing up and general cleaning. Home to many major labour-saving devices, such as the washing machine, dishwasher and food processor, it may need to accommodate several family members at the same time and to double as a breakfast or snack room. Easy access to other eating areas, such as a dining room, may be needed, so that cooked food reaches the table quickly. A large serving hatch between the kitchen and dining room may be the ideal solution, providing a practical and visual link.

The bathroom

In a large household, a second bathroom is a modern necessity, and builders' merchants stock all types of space-saving units with this in mind. If your main bathroom is fitted out traditionally (i.e. with a bath), a shower room would be a good idea, along with a second toilet, possibly incorporated in a downstairs cloakroom. If space precludes all these options, another possibility would be to divide the toilet off from the rest of the bathroom.

Interconnecting spaces

In an ideal world the home you inhabit would grow and change with you and your family. This is possible if the house layout is flexible. Corridors that have a decorative scheme encouraging adjacent areas to interact, rather than divorcing one from another, are a particularly good start.

The décor in any area becomes more interesting if flexible design allows the occupants to see through to another, different space.

Linking rooms does not necessarily have to mean sacrificing privacy, either. Decorative screens can be used to temporarily isolate parts of the open space as and when you wish.

If you have the room to create open spaces in this way, however, you should try to avoid overcompensating by adding too much furniture – an understandable temptation.

Minimalism will not be an option for a family unit, of course, but too much clutter will rapidly reduce or destroy any feeling of spaciousness that you endeavour to create.

Opposite ideas often work well together. For example, a small apartment will appear larger if it is visually sparse. By contrast, a large loft apartment benefits from an aggressive colour scheme that is used to reduce the overwhelming impact of the space.

LEFT: This bedroom in the loft area of the house lends itself to several purposes at once: a sleeping area, with storage in the foreground, a sewing area and, at the back of the room, a shower area.

The space on this floor has been utilised to make a home office on a separate floor, which divides up the living and working areas.

Accommodating the new

Period housing has many features that can live happily alongside modern innovations in this technological age, and it is worth assessing how modernisation will work in your home without removing original features. In addition, you will need to consider how the requirements of the household members will be met by your refurbishment choices.

RIGHT: **A small space can be successfully multifunctional, as a bedroom, washing area and work unit, if it is well planned and the various components form an integral whole that is pleasing to the eye.**

A hall area ideally needs to be reasonably spacious, to have a floor surface that is easily cleaned and plenty of room for hanging up coats and storing umbrellas, boots and shoes.

Original features and new technology

Technology can work in any surroundings, and stylish period features don't have to make way for contemporary interiors to accommodate innovations. Original fireplaces, skirtings, cornices and decorative mouldings can all be updated by adventurous colour scheming, irrespective of their Georgian, Regency, Victorian or Edwardian origin.

Water and electricity supplies in older properties must meet modern standards and regulations, but they can be largely hidden away, and the growing reproduction marketplace supplies period-style radiators and switch surrounds. Brand-name paint manufacturers offer a range of period colours, and architectural

salvage yards are full of period pieces for the bargain-hunter.

Opposites can work very well together. A digital sound system can look and sound superb in an elaborate Victorian Sunday room. If you are considering a large-scale refurbishment programme, keep your mind and your options open to the possibilities for accommodating new technology in a traditional setting.

Unique family needs

Along with considering room function, period styles and linked colour schemes, you also need to assess requirements that are unique to your family. Every person who lives in the property should be allowed an input because any form of alteration or decoration is a family affair.

Needs alter as the years pass. Children who once shared a room will want to move apart,

eventually to leave altogether. Elderly relatives may join the household. Flexibility is crucial. It may be difficult and time-consuming to adapt a house to fit the occupants, but equally it may be difficult to change the habits of a lifetime to suit the layout of a property.

Here are some points to consider:

- Is there adequate provision in the entrance hall or lobby for wet outdoor clothes, boots and/or sporting equipment?
- Can this area be cleaned easily?
- Is there space in this area to put down shopping items temporarily, while a cab is being paid off or a vehicle is being unloaded?
- Can late-night arrivals get to their rooms directly without disturbing the rest of the household?
- Do all the sleeping areas have easy access to both the bathroom and the toilet?
- Can a meal cooked in the kitchen be served in the dining area easily and quickly?
- Does the kitchen have a back door, to allow deliveries to arrive and garbage to be removed easily? Is this access protected from the weather?
- Can you view the rest of the property, and any garden where the children may be playing, from the kitchen?
- Is there enough storage space and hobby space?
- Can a bedroom double up as a study area or home office during the daytime?
- If a workshop with power tools, such as a garage area, is open to everyone in the house, is it safe?
- Are all potentially dangerous tools locked away?
- If you have a pet, is it catered for in all weathers?

Nobody knows more about your family circumstances than you do, so adapt the questionnaire to your own situation. Put your requirements in writing. They will provide invaluable guidance when you come to make final decisions.

ORIGINAL FITTINGS

Period fireplaces have an innate charm, and an old fireplace surround can often be adapted to take modern fittings and painted in either traditional or modern colours. In the summer, grates can be filled with pine cones and massed with greenery, so that they do not look redundant at this time of year.

Old radiators still have a certain appeal, and can often be bought at architectural salvage yards and brought back to life. Alternatively you can purchase a reproduction radiator and enjoy all the benefits of modern technology with the aesthetic values of another era.

Major or minor changes?

If your decision involves changing the function of a particular area, consider how major those changes will be. A bedroom to be used as a study, for example, will require largely cosmetic changes, such as new shelving, a worktop for a computer and décor to be approved by the new inhabitant. However, enlarging a kitchen by, say, connecting it directly to a utility room may involve levelling one of the floors for retiling, removing doors and matching panelled interiors. Any major kitchen or bathroom work will involve water facilities and the services of a plumber, so consult a local tradesperson before final redesign decisions are made. Electrics are another consideration. Are there enough outlets, and are they in the right place? Is the lighting good enough, especially if the house is old? Unless you have experience in this field, seek the advice of a professional electrician. Major disruptive work needs to be completed before any cosmetic details can be started.

Making plans

Whether your plan is complex or simple at this stage, whether you intend to divide up a room space or merely paint a floor, you will find a detailed plan on paper makes life a lot easier. It doesn't have to be a work of art, but it does need to be accurate. If you have a computer with suitable software, you can draw up your plans and alter them using a grid system. You might even be able to put together a three-dimensional drawing.

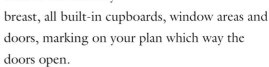

necessary, and note down the sizes of the chimney breast, all built-in cupboards, window areas and doors, marking on your plan which way the doors open.

You will find it easier to write down initial measurements on a rough sketch. You can also add items that cannot be easily changed, such as radiator positions and pipe runs, electric outlets and light fittings to this first drawing, even if they are not relevant to the final scheme.

ABOVE: **The essential tools required for measuring a room are graph paper, some coloured pencils, a notepad and pen, a clear plastic rule, a pair of scissors, a retractable steel measure and a calculator.**

RIGHT: **Mark on the plan the room's basic dimensions, noting in particular any unusual shapes that distort the room's appearance, and all the doors, windows and other features such as cupboards.**

Measuring up a room

To measure up a room, use a retractable steel measure of at least 5m/16½ft total length, with a lever to lock the tape at any given distance. Adding distances together from shorter tape measures, or using cloth tapes that are prone to sag, leads to inaccurate figures.

Measure the basic dimensions of the room first – the wall height and length. Measure the room from corner to corner to confirm that it is square, or at least square enough for your purposes. Add on any bay window and alcove areas, where

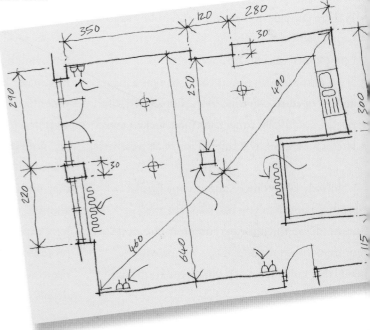

Transferring to graph paper

Using a pencil transfer your plan from rough sketch to graph paper and scale the area to size using the squares. Include only the items that you consider relevant from your comprehensive measurements. Simplify the plan as much as possible to reduce the risk of errors. If your room is furnished, or if you know what items of furniture will eventually be included, then represent these objects with small pieces of card cut to scale. You will be able to rearrange items of furniture at will, to establish their best position and to make maximum use of the available space.

Draw in shelving systems or new cupboards to go in alcoves, change access doors, and so on, until you are happy that the plan is complete.

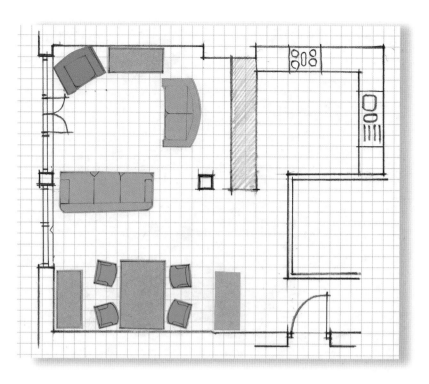

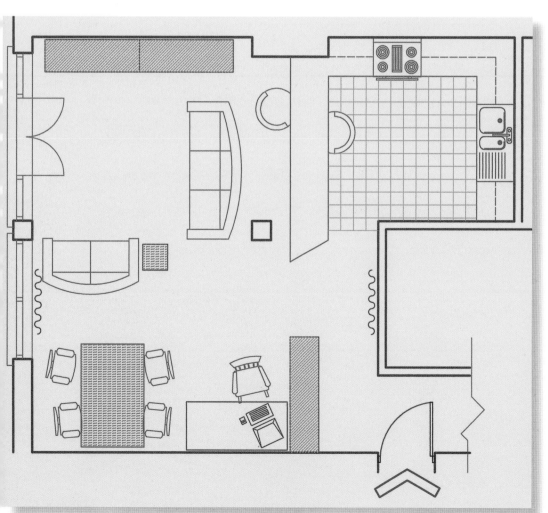

ABOVE: **A plan comes to life when the items of furniture are coloured in and you can see how they relate to one another and how they fill the space. Try moving them around to ascertain the ideal configuration.**

LEFT: **Because of the positions of doors, windows and chimney breasts there are only so many combinations that will work in any given space. With trial and error you should finally arrive at the perfect solution.**

Colour

Choosing the correct colour scheme for your home is vital
to your sense of comfort and well-being. Individual tastes in colour
are, of course, highly subjective, but there are also several important
objective factors involved in the selection of colour schemes. In this
chapter we look at the colour wheel, which will help in choosing
contrasting and complementary colour schemes, and also discuss the
importance of natural light, the psychological effects of particular
colours and the visual tricks that can be achieved through careful
colour scheming. Successful use of colour has the potential to
transform rooms in an exciting and gratifying way, and in many
instances involves no great expense to you, so it is well worth
taking your time considering all the choices available.